BANANAS

BANANAS

southwater

This edition is published by Southwater

Distributed in the UK by
The Manning Partnership
251–253 London Road East
Batheaston
Bath BA1 7RL
UK
tel. (0044) 01225 852 727
fax (0044) 01225 852 852

Distributed in Australia by
Sandstone Publishing
Unit 1, 360 Norton Street
Leichhardt
New South Wales 2040
Australia
tel. (0061) 2 9560 7888
fax (0061) 2 9560 7488

Distributed in New Zealand by
Five Mile Press NZ
PO Box 33-1071
Takapuna
Auckland 9
New Zealand
tel. (0064) 9 4444 144
fax (0064) 9 4444 518

Southwater is an imprint of Anness Publishing Limited
© 1997, 2000 Anness Publishing Limited

1 3 5 7 9 10 8 6 4 2

Publisher Joanna Lorenz
Senior Cookery Editor Linda Fraser
Project Editor Anne Hildyard
Designer Bill Mason
Illustrations Anna Koska

Photographers Karl Adamson, Steve Baxter, James Duncan, Amanda Heywood,
Don Last, Patrick McLeavey and Thomas Odulate
Recipes Kit Chan, Christine France, Sarah Gates, Shirley Gill, Rosamund Grant, Manisha
Kanani, Sallie Morris, Anne Sheasby and Steven Wheeler
Food for photography Carla Capalbo, Elizabeth Wolf-Cohen, Joanne Craig, Jane Hartshorn,
Wendy Lee, Jane Stevenson and Judy Williams
Stylists Madeleine Brehaut, Hilary Guy, Blake Minton, Kirsty Rawlings and Fiona Tillett

For all recipes, quantities are given in both metric and imperial measures and, where
appropriate, measures are also given in standard cups and spoons. Follow one set, but not a
mixture, because they are not interchangeable.

Previously published as *Bananas: A Book of Recipes*

Contents

INTRODUCTION

Bananas are the ultimate healthy, high-energy, convenience food. Neatly packaged in their attractive easy-to-open skins, the sweet-tasting fruit with their delicate aroma are packed with vitamins, minerals and complexion-enhancing pectin and are high in energy-giving starch. Bananas originated in South-East Asia and have grown in the tropics since ancient times. Hundreds of different varieties of bananas flourish in many tropical countries, from the West Indies and Africa to South-East Asia, South America and the Canaries. The very sight of huge "hands" of bananas pointing upwards through the elongated green leaves of the banana plant is enough to conjure up a feeling of exoticism. All sweet bananas are delicious eaten raw, but their versatile flesh is equally good made into ice cream, soufflés and trifles. They combine well with other ingredients from tropical regions, especially brown sugar, rum, coconut, mangoes, passion fruit and pineapple.

Bananas can also be used as a vegetable. You might mistake green-skinned plantains for unripe sweet bananas, but they are starchier and contain less sugar, and are almost always served cooked in savoury dishes. They can be boiled, fried or mashed like potatoes and are an essential ingredient of many West Indian and African dishes. They have a particular affinity with white fish and bacon. Every part of the banana can be used in cooking, even the skin, which forms a protective wrapping for baked bananas, while the leaves make neat aromatic packets to enclose a filling.

Because they come from the tropics, bananas are available all year round. They are picked and exported while they are still green, and are ripened in storage. You can buy bananas in all stages of ripeness, from hard and green to soft and yellow mottled with brown, but they ripen very quickly, turning brown with speckled yellow flesh which is really only suitable for cooking.

This book begins with an introduction to the various bananas and plantains available in the shops and guides you through choosing and preparing them. Two chapters of exciting savoury dishes follow, including exotic starters, snacks and main courses from Africa, Thailand and the Caribbean. Finally, dessert bananas make their appearance in many attractive guises, from healthy tropical banana fruit salad to irresistible chocolate cake with banana sauce, and including exotic combinations like Brazilian coffee bananas, hot bananas with rum and raisins and banana and passion fruit whip. All these recipes reveal the versatility of one of the world's favourite exotic fruits.

Types of Bananas

Dessert Bananas

Standard dessert bananas are long, curved fruit with yellow skins, turning to speckled brown as they ripen. Unripe bananas have green skins or greenish tips. They are difficult to peel and are not pleasant to eat, as they have a crunchy texture and make your mouth pucker. The most common type of dessert banana is Cavendish, which has many sub-varieties. However, unless you are a banana expert, it is virtually impossible to differentiate between them. All dessert bananas are delicious raw or cooked.

Apple Bananas

These tiny yellow bananas from Colombia are about half the size of ordinary bananas. They have golden flesh with a faint aroma and flavour of apple.

Green Bananas

Large green bananas can be cooked in much the same way as potatoes and are often served as a substitute, although they have a blander flavour. They have crisp flesh which can be boiled, mashed or fried in butter. Fried green banana rings are particularly good served with white fish or in a curry.

Banana Leaves

Banana leaves are shaped like elongated fans, with long straight veins running from the centre to the edges. Whole, unblemished banana leaves are soft and malleable, and can be folded or rolled into parcels to keep the filling moist and succulent. They impart a delicate flavour to the food and look very attractive.

Plantains

Yellow and green plantains look like large bananas, but their shape is longer and flatter. They have firm pinkish flesh which contains more starch but is less sweet than that of dessert bananas. As the plantain ripens, the flesh becomes darker and sweeter and can be used in desserts. However, it is more usual to serve plantains as a vegetable. Very firm plantains can be thinly sliced and deep-fried as an unusual alternative to potato crisps.

Dried Bananas

Drying intensifies the sweetness of bananas. Dried bananas are usually sold as bars; they are dark, sticky and very sweet. Eaten on their own, they make a chewy but nutritious and energizing snack.

Unripe plantain

Green bananas

Dried bananas

Ripe plantain

Apple bananas

Dessert bananas

Banana leaf

$\mathcal{B}$ASIC $\mathcal{T}$ECHNIQUES

CHOOSING BANANAS

• Uniformly green fruit is unripe and almost inedible.

• Bananas with green-tinged ends are slightly unripe, with a crisp texture and a refreshing taste.

• Perfectly ripe bananas are uniformly yellow and the flesh is soft and sweet.

• As bananas continue to ripen, brown speckles appear on the skin until it is covered with brown mottling. At this stage, the flesh is very sweet and soft and perfect for mashing for mousses or banana sandwiches, for example.

• The final stage, when the skin is dark brown all over, is the last chance to eat the banana. The flesh will have almost collapsed and tastes like fermenting honey. A banana which has reached this stage of over-ripeness is best used for cooking.

PREPARING BANANAS

PEELING BANANAS
Strip the skin in complete sections from ripe bananas from the stalk end. Remove any white threads from the flesh before eating or using the bananas in cooking.

SLICING BANANAS
For fruit salads and trifles, slice the bananas crossways into rings. If you are baking the bananas, slice them lengthways, then cut them in half again into chunks.

DIPPING IN LEMON JUICE
After peeling and slicing bananas, dip them into fresh lemon juice to prevent the flesh discolouring. Turn the banana slices in the juice to coat them on all sides.

PEELING PLANTAINS

Using a small, sharp knife, top and tail the plantains. Discard the ends and stalks and cut the plantains in half crossways.

Using a small, sharp knife, slit the skin of each piece of plantain, in a few places, along the natural ridges. Take care not to cut through the flesh.

Ease up the edge of the skin and run the tip of your thumb along the plantain pieces, lifting the skin. Peel off the skin and discard it.

SESAME TOFFEE BANANAS

Serves 4

The contrast between the crunchy coating and the soft banana within is irresistible.

Cut four peeled bananas into chunks and brush with lemon juice. Sift 50g/2oz flour and a pinch of salt into a bowl and add 1 egg and 120ml/4fl oz/½ cup milk. Stir to make a batter.

Put 15ml/1 tbsp groundnut oil, 225g/8oz caster sugar, 50ml/2fl oz/¼ cup water and 30ml/2 tbsp sesame seeds in a saucepan and heat gently until the sugar dissolves. Increase the heat and boil for 10–15 minutes to make a deep golden caramel.

Heat a pan of vegetable oil to 190°C/375°F for deep-frying. Dip the bananas in the batter and fry them in batches until puffed up. Remove and drain on kitchen paper. Using two forks, dip the banana fritters into the sesame caramel to coat them all over.

Appetizers, Snacks and Side Dishes

Bananas and plantains add delicious flavour and texture to a variety of exotic dishes, such as crunchy assorted plantain appetizers, steamed fish parcels and green bananas and yam.

PLANTAIN AND CORN CHOWDER

Unlike dessert bananas, plantains are always cooked. Firm and starchy, they make a delicious soup.

Serves 4

25g/1oz/2 tbsp butter or margarine

1 onion, finely chopped

1 garlic clove, crushed

275g/10oz yellow plantains, peeled
   and sliced

1 large tomato, skinned and chopped

175g/6oz/1 cup sweetcorn kernels

5ml/1 tsp crushed dried tarragon

900ml/1½ pints/3¾ cups vegetable
   or chicken stock

1 fresh green chilli, seeded
   and chopped

pinch of grated nutmeg

salt and ground black pepper

Melt the butter or margarine in a saucepan over a medium heat, add the onion and garlic and fry for 3–4 minutes until the onion is soft.

Add the sliced plantains, tomato and sweetcorn and cook for 5 minutes.

Stir in the tarragon, vegetable or chicken stock and chilli, with salt and pepper to taste. Bring to the boil, then lower the heat and simmer for about 10 minutes or until the plantains are just tender. Stir in the nutmeg and serve the soup at once.

STEAMED BANANA LEAF PARCELS

Very neat and delicate, these steamed seafood packets from Thailand make an excellent starter or light lunch.

Serves 4

225g/8oz crab meat

50g/2oz peeled prawns, chopped

6 drained water chestnuts, chopped

30ml/2 tbsp chopped bamboo shoots

15ml/1 tbsp chopped spring onion

5ml/1 tsp chopped fresh root ginger

30ml/2 tbsp soy sauce

15ml/1 tbsp fish sauce

12 rice sheets

banana leaves, for lining steamer

oil for brushing

2 spring onions, shredded, 2 fresh red chillies, seeded and sliced, and coriander leaves, to garnish

COOK'S TIP
The seafood packets will spread out when cooked so be sure to space them well apart in the steamer to prevent them sticking together.

Combine the crab meat, chopped prawns, chestnuts, bamboo shoots, spring onion and ginger in a bowl. Mix well, then add 15ml/1 tbsp of the soy sauce and all the fish sauce. Stir until blended.

Take a rice sheet and dip it in warm water. Place it on a flat surface and leave for a few seconds to soften.

Place a spoonful of the filling in the centre of the sheet and fold into a square packet. Repeat with the rest of the rice sheets and seafood mixture.

Use banana leaves to line a steamer, then brush them with oil. Place the packets, seam side down, on the leaves and steam over a high heat for 6–8 minutes or until the filling is cooked. Transfer to a plate and garnish with the spring onions, chillies and coriander leaves.

ASSIETTE OF PLANTAINS

This mélange of succulent sweet and savoury plantains makes a delicious crunchy appetizer.

Serves 4

vegetable oil, for shallow frying

2 green plantains

1 yellow plantain

½ onion

pinch of garlic granules

salt and cayenne pepper

Heat the oil in a large frying pan over a medium heat. While the oil is heating, peel one of the green plantains and cut into very thin rounds using a vegetable peeler. Fry the plantain rounds in the oil for about 3 minutes, turning until golden brown. Drain on kitchen paper and keep warm.

Coarsely grate the remaining green plantain on to a plate. Slice the onion into wafer-thin shreds and mix with the grated plantain. Heat a little more oil in the frying pan and fry handfuls of the mixture for 2–3 minutes, until golden, turning once. Drain on kitchen paper and keep warm.

Peel the yellow plantain, cut it in half lengthways and dice. Sprinkle with the garlic granules and cayenne pepper. Heat a little more oil in the frying pan and fry the plantain until evenly golden brown. Drain on kitchen paper and then arrange the three varieties of cooked plantains in shallow dishes. Sprinkle with salt and serve as a snack.

FRIED YELLOW PLANTAINS

When plantains are ripe, they turn yellow and become sweeter, but not as sweet as dessert bananas. This makes them the perfect accompaniment to grills and roasts.

Serves 4

2 yellow plantains
oil, for shallow frying
finely snipped fresh chives or finely
* chopped fresh mixed herbs,*
* to garnish*

Using a small sharp knife, top and tail the plantains, and cut each of them in half. Slit the skin only, along the natural ridges of each piece of plantain. Ease up the edge of the skin and run the tip of your thumb along the plantains, lifting the skin. Peel away the skin and slice the plantains in half lengthways.

Heat a little oil in a large frying pan and fry the plantain slices for 2–3 minutes on each side until golden brown. Do not overcook as they can become rather dry and starchy.

When the plantains are golden brown and crisp, lift out the slices using a slotted spoon. Drain the plantains on kitchen paper to remove excess oil. Serve hot or cold, sprinkled with finely snipped chives or with finely chopped fresh mixed herbs. Serve the fried plantains with grilled or roast meat, fish or vegetarian dishes.

COOK'S TIP
Look for plantains at vegetable markets and large supermarkets. You can use bananas as a substitute, but they tend to become rather too soft when cooked.

GREEN BANANAS AND YAM

For a tantalizing taste of the tropics, try this unusual vegetable and banana medley.

Serves 3–4

4 green bananas, peeled and halved

450g/1lb white yam, peeled and cut
into pieces

1 thyme sprig

40g/1½oz creamed coconut, cubed

salt and ground black pepper

chopped fresh thyme and thyme
sprigs, to garnish

COOK'S TIP
*Creamed coconut is available
in blocks from oriental food
stores and some supermarkets.
It can be thinned by mixing it
with a little water to make
coconut milk.*

Bring 900ml/1½ pints/3¾ cups water to the boil in a large saucepan, lower the heat and add the green bananas and yam. Simmer gently for about 10 minutes.

Add the thyme and coconut, with salt and pepper to taste. Bring back to the boil and cook over a medium heat until the yam and banana are tender.

Using a slotted spoon, transfer the yam and banana to a plate. Continue cooking the coconut milk, stirring frequently, until thick and creamy.

When the sauce is ready, return the vegetables to the pan and heat through. Spoon into a warmed serving dish, sprinkle with chopped thyme and garnish with thyme sprigs.

YAM AND PLANTAIN FU FU

Small, savoury and packed with flavour, serve these yam and plantain balls with casseroles and stews.

Serves 4

450g/1lb white yam

2 green plantains

15g/¹⁄₂oz/1 tbsp butter or margarine

salt and ground black or white
* pepper*

flat-leaved parsley, to garnish

Peel, wash and slice the yam. Place in a saucepan and pour in lightly salted cold water to cover. Cut the green plantains in half, slit along the natural ridges in three places and remove the skins. Add to the yam, bring to the boil and cook for 25 minutes until the vegetables are tender.

Drain the vegetables and place in a blender or food processor. Add the butter or margarine, season well with salt and pepper, and process until smooth and lump free.

Scrape the fu fu into a bowl, then take small handfuls and shape into balls. Reheat in a low oven or in the microwave. Garnish with parsley and serve.

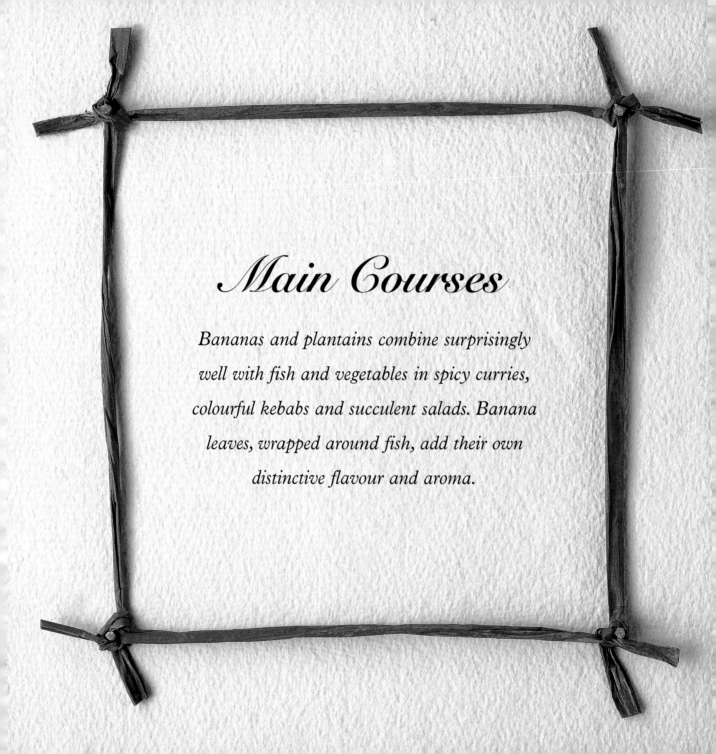

Main Courses

*Bananas and plantains combine surprisingly
well with fish and vegetables in spicy curries,
colourful kebabs and succulent salads. Banana
leaves, wrapped around fish, add their own
distinctive flavour and aroma.*

BANANA CURRY

The sweetness of the bananas combines well with the spices used to produce a mild, sweet curry.

Serves 4

4 under-ripe bananas

30ml/2 tbsp ground coriander

15ml/1 tbsp ground cumin

5ml/1 tsp chilli powder

2.5ml/½ tsp salt

1.5ml/¼ tsp ground turmeric

5ml/1 tsp granulated sugar

15ml/1 tbsp gram flour

45ml/3 tbsp chopped fresh coriander

90ml/6 tbsp corn oil

1.5ml/¼ tsp cumin seeds

1.5ml/¼ tsp black mustard seeds

fresh coriander sprigs, to garnish

chappatis, to serve

COOK'S TIP

Choose bananas that are slightly under-ripe so that they retain their shape and do not become unpleasantly mushy when they are cooked.

Trim the bananas, leaving the skin on, and cut each into three equal pieces. Make a lengthways slit in each piece of banana, without cutting through.

Mix the ground coriander, cumin, chilli powder, salt, turmeric, sugar, gram flour and chopped coriander in a soup plate. Stir in 15ml/1 tbsp of the oil. Carefully stuff each piece of banana with the spice mixture, taking care not to break them in half.

Heat the remaining oil in a large heavy-based saucepan and fry the cumin and mustard seeds for 2 minutes or until they begin to splutter. Add the bananas and toss gently in the oil. Cover and simmer over a low heat for 15 minutes, stirring from time to time, until the bananas are soft, but not mushy. Garnish with the fresh coriander and serve with warm chappatis.

PLANTAIN AND VEGETABLE KEBABS

Tasty and colourful, these kebabs make a delightful main course for vegetarians or can be served as a side dish.

Serves 4

115g/4oz pumpkin, peeled and cubed

1 red onion, cut into wedges

1 small courgette, sliced

1 yellow plantain, sliced

1 aubergine, diced

½ red pepper, seeded and diced

½ green pepper, seeded and diced

12 button mushrooms, trimmed

60ml/4 tbsp lemon juice

60ml/4 tbsp olive or sunflower oil

45–60ml/3–4 tbsp soy sauce

150ml/¼ pint/⅔ cup tomato juice

1 fresh green chilli, seeded
   and chopped

½ onion, grated

3 garlic cloves, crushed

7.5ml/1½ tsp dried
   tarragon, crushed

4ml/¾ tsp each dried basil, dried
   thyme and ground cinnamon

25g/1oz/2 tbsp butter

300ml/½ pint/1¼ cups vegetable stock

freshly ground black pepper

Place the pumpkin in a small bowl and cover with boiling water. Blanch for 2–3 minutes, then drain, refresh under cold water, drain again and tip into a large bowl. Add the red onion, courgette, plantain, aubergine, peppers and mushrooms.

Mix the lemon juice, oil, soy sauce, tomato juice, chilli, grated onion, garlic, herbs, cinnamon and black pepper in a jug. Pour over the vegetables. Toss well, then set aside in a cool place to marinate for 3–4 hours.

Drain the vegetables and thread them alternately on to eight skewers. Grill under a low heat for about 15 minutes, turning the kebabs frequently, until golden brown. Baste occasionally with the marinade to keep the vegetables moist.

Place the remaining marinade, butter and stock in a pan and bring to the boil. Lower the heat and simmer for 10 minutes to cook the onion and reduce the sauce. Pour into a serving jug. Arrange the vegetable skewers on a plate. Serve with a rice dish or salad.

PLANTAIN AND GREEN BANANA SALAD

Cooking plantains and bananas in their skins helps to retain the soft texture so that they absorb all the flavour of the dressing.

Serves 4

2 ripe yellow plantains

3 green bananas

1 garlic clove, crushed

1 red onion

15–30ml/1–2 tbsp chopped
  fresh coriander

45ml/3 tbsp sunflower oil

25ml/1½ tbsp malt vinegar

salt and coarse-grain black pepper

Slit the plantains and bananas lengthways along their natural ridges, then cut in half and place in a large saucepan. Pour in water to cover, add a little salt and bring to the boil.

Boil the plantains and bananas gently for 20 minutes until tender, then drain well. When they are cool enough to handle, peel and cut them into medium-sized slices.

Put the plantain and banana slices into a bowl and add the crushed garlic, turning to mix.

Cut the onion in half and slice it thinly. Add to the bowl with the chopped fresh coriander, oil and vinegar. Add salt and pepper to taste. Toss to mix, then serve.

COOK'S TIP
Red onions are mild and sweet, so they are ideal for mixing in salads and for adding extra flavour to sandwiches.

SPINACH PLANTAIN ROUNDS

This delectable way of serving plantains is a little fiddly to make, but well worth the trouble. The plantains must be ripe, but still firm.

Serves 4

2 large yellow plantains, peeled
oil, for frying
30ml/2 tbsp butter
25g/1oz/1 tbsp finely chopped onion
2 garlic cloves, crushed
450g/1lb fresh spinach, chopped
pinch of freshly grated nutmeg
1 egg, beaten
wholemeal flour, for dusting
salt and ground black pepper

Using a small, sharp knife, carefully cut each plantain lengthways into four slices. Heat a little oil in a large frying pan and fry the slices on both sides until pale gold in colour, but not fully cooked. Lift out and drain on kitchen paper and reserve the oil in the frying pan.

Melt the butter in a saucepan and sauté the onion and garlic for 2–3 minutes until the onion is soft. Add the spinach and nutmeg, with salt and pepper to taste. Cover and cook for about 5 minutes until the spinach has reduced. Cool, then tip into a sieve, and press out any excess moisture.

Curl the plantain slices into rings and secure each ring with a wooden cocktail stick. Pack each ring with a little of the spinach mixture.

Place the egg and flour in two separate shallow dishes. Add a little more oil to the frying pan, if necessary, and heat until moderately hot. Dip the plantain rings in the egg and then in the flour and fry on both sides for 1–2 minutes until golden brown. Drain on kitchen paper and serve hot or cold.

COOK'S TIP
If fresh spinach is not available, use frozen spinach. Thaw completely and drain thoroughly in a sieve before cooking.

SPICY PLANTAINS WITH YAM

This tomato-flavoured plantain dish is a perfect partner for a spicy meat or fish stew.

Serves 4

2 green plantains

450g/1lb white yam

2 tomatoes, skinned and chopped

1 fresh red chilli, seeded and chopped

1 onion, chopped

½ vegetable stock cube

15ml/1 tbsp palm oil

15ml/1 tbsp tomato purée

salt

VARIATION

Use 2 leeks or shallots instead of the onion, and substitute diced marrow or courgettes for the yam.

Peel the plantains and cut into six rounds, then peel and dice the yam. Place in a large saucepan. Add 600ml/1 pint/2½ cups water, bring to the boil and cook for 5 minutes.

Add the tomatoes, chilli and onion to the pan and simmer for about 10 minutes, then crumble in the stock cube, stir well, cover and simmer for another 5 minutes.

Stir in the oil and tomato purée and continue cooking for about 5 minutes until the plantains are tender. Season with salt and pour into a warmed serving dish. Serve immediately.

BAKED FISH IN BANANA LEAVES

Fish baked in banana leaves is particularly succulent and flavourful. This is a great dish for barbecuing.

Serves 4

250ml/8 fl oz/1 cup coconut milk
30ml/2 tbsp red curry paste
45ml/3 tbsp fish sauce
30ml/2 tbsp caster sugar
5 kaffir lime leaves, torn
4 fish fillets, about 175g/6oz each
175g/6oz mixed vegetables, such as
  carrots or leeks, finely shredded
4 banana leaves

For the garnish

30ml/2 tbsp shredded spring onions
2 fresh red chillies, finely sliced

Combine the coconut milk, curry paste, fish sauce, sugar and kaffir lime leaves in a shallow dish. Add the fish and marinate for 15–30 minutes. Preheat the oven to 200°C/ 400°F/Gas 6.

Mix the selected vegetables together and place a quarter of the mixture on top of a banana leaf. Place a fish fillet on top of each and moisten it with a little of the marinade.

Wrap the fish up by turning in the sides and ends of the leaf and securing the package with cocktail sticks. Repeat with the rest of the leaves, vegetables and fish.

Bake for 20–25 minutes or until the fish is cooked. Alternatively, cook under the grill or in a hinged grill over a barbecue. Just before serving, garnish the fish with a sprinkling of spring onions and sliced red chillies.

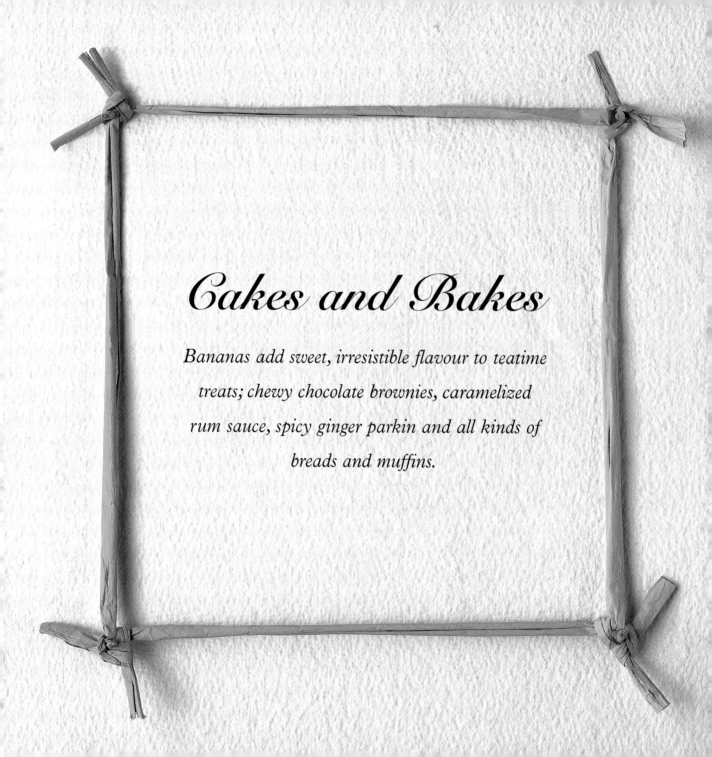

Cakes and Bakes

Bananas add sweet, irresistible flavour to teatime treats; chewy chocolate brownies, caramelized rum sauce, spicy ginger parkin and all kinds of breads and muffins.

CHOCOLATE AND BANANA BROWNIES

Bananas give brownies a delicious flavour and keep them marvellously moist.

Makes 9

75ml/5 tbsp cocoa powder

15ml/1 tbsp caster sugar

75ml/5 tbsp milk

3 large bananas, mashed

*175g/6oz/1 cup soft light
   brown sugar*

5ml/1 tsp vanilla essence

5 egg whites

75g/3oz/³⁄₄ cup self-raising flour

50g/2oz/²⁄₃ cup oat bran

15ml/1 tbsp icing sugar, for dusting

COOK'S TIP
*Store these brownies in an
airtight container for one day
before eating them – their
flavour becomes stronger and
improves with keeping.*

Preheat the oven to 180°C/350°F/Gas 4. Line a 20cm/8in square baking tin with non-stick baking paper. In a bowl, mix the cocoa powder and caster sugar with the milk. Add the bananas, brown sugar and vanilla essence. Mix well.

In a mixing bowl, beat the egg whites lightly with a fork. Add the chocolate mixture and continue to beat well. Sift the flour over the mixture and fold in with the oat bran. Pour into the prepared tin.

Bake for 40 minutes or until firm. Cool in the tin for 10 minutes, then turn out on to a wire rack and cool completely. Cut into nine wedges and dust lightly with icing sugar before serving.

CHOCOLATE CAKE WITH BANANA SAUCE

Caramelized banana and rum sauce tastes superb with wedges of chocolate cake.

Serves 6

*115g/4oz plain chocolate, broken
    into squares*

*115g/4oz/½ cup unsalted butter, at
    room temperature*

15ml/1 tbsp instant coffee powder

5 eggs, separated

225g/8oz/1 cup granulated sugar

115g/4oz/1 cup plain flour

5ml/1 tsp ground cinnamon

For the sauce

4 ripe bananas

60ml/4 tbsp soft light brown sugar

15ml/1 tbsp lemon juice

175ml/6fl oz/¾ cup whipping cream

15ml/1 tbsp rum (optional)

Preheat the oven to 180°C/350°F/Gas 4. Grease a 20cm/8in round cake tin. Bring a small saucepan of water to the boil. Remove it from the heat and place a heatproof bowl on top. Add the chocolate and butter to the bowl and leave until melted, stirring occasionally. Stir in the coffee powder and set aside.

Mix the egg yolks and granulated sugar in a bowl. Beat by hand or with an electric mixer until thick and lemon-coloured. Add the chocolate mixture and beat on low speed for just long enough to blend the mixtures evenly.

Sift the flour and cinnamon into a bowl. In another bowl, beat the egg whites to stiff peaks. Fold a spoon of egg white into the chocolate mixture to lighten it. Fold in the remaining egg white in batches, alternating with the sifted flour mixture.

Pour the mixture into the prepared tin. Bake for 40–50 minutes or until a skewer inserted in the centre comes out clean. Turn out on to a wire rack.

Preheat the grill. Make the sauce. Slice the bananas into a shallow, flameproof dish. Add the brown sugar and lemon juice and stir to mix. Place under the grill and cook, stirring occasionally, for about 8 minutes until the sugar is caramelized and bubbling. Mash the bananas into the sauce until almost smooth. Stir in the cream and rum, if using. Slice the cake and serve it warm, with the sauce.

BANANA MUFFINS

Make plenty of these delectable treats – banana muffins are irresistible at any time of the day.

Makes 10

225g/8oz/2 cups plain flour

5ml/1 tsp baking powder

5ml/1 tsp bicarbonate of soda

1.5ml/¼ tsp salt

1.5ml/¼ tsp grated nutmeg

2.5ml/½ tsp ground cinnamon

3 large ripe bananas

1 egg

*50g/2oz/⅓ cup soft dark
    brown sugar*

60ml/4 tbsp vegetable oil

40g/1½oz/¼ cup raisins

Preheat the oven to 190°C/375°F/Gas 5. Line 10 muffin cups with paper liners or grease them lightly. Sift the flour, baking powder, bicarbonate of soda, salt, nutmeg and cinnamon into a bowl. Set aside.

Mash the bananas in a mixing bowl until creamy. Using a hand-held electric mixer, beat in the egg, sugar and oil. Add the dry ingredients and mix until just blended. Stir in the raisins.

Fill the muffin cups two-thirds full. Bake for 20–25 minutes or until the tops spring back when lightly touched. Transfer the muffins to a wire rack to cool slightly. Serve warm.

COOK'S TIP

If there are any empty cups in the muffin tray when you have used up the mixture, fill them with water before placing the tray in the oven to ensure that the muffins bake evenly.

BANANA GINGER PARKIN

Bananas and ginger make a winning combination. This parkin actually improves with keeping.

Makes 12 bars

200g/7oz/1¾ cups plain flour

10ml/2 tsp bicarbonate of soda

10ml/2 tsp ground ginger

150g/5oz/1¼ cups medium oatmeal

60ml/4 tbsp dark muscovado sugar

75g/3oz/6 tbsp butter or margarine

150g/5oz/⅔ cup golden syrup

1 egg, beaten

3 ripe bananas, mashed

75g/3oz/¾ cup icing sugar

stem ginger, to decorate

COOK'S TIP

This is a nutritious, energy-giving cake that is an excellent choice for packed lunches, as it does not break up or crumble very easily.

Preheat the oven to 160°C/325°F/Gas 3. Grease and line a 28 x 18cm/11 x 7in cake tin. Sift the flour, bicarbonate of soda and ginger into a bowl, then stir in the oatmeal.

Melt the sugar, butter or margarine and syrup in a saucepan, then stir into the flour mixture. Beat in the egg and mashed bananas.

Spoon the mixture into the tin and bake for about 1 hour, or until firm to the touch. Allow to cool in the tin, then turn out and cut into bars.

Sift the icing sugar into a bowl and stir in just enough water to make a smooth, runny icing. Drizzle the icing over each square and top the parkin with slices of stem ginger.

Banana and Lemon Cake

Light, moist and flavoursome, this cake keeps very well and is everybody's favourite.

Serves 8-10

250g/9oz/2¼ cups plain flour

6.5ml/1¼ tsp baking powder

pinch of salt

115g/4oz/½ cup unsalted butter, at
    room temperature

200g/7oz/scant 1 cup caster sugar

75g/3oz/⅓ cup soft light brown sugar

2 eggs

2.5ml/½ tsp grated lemon rind

225g/8oz/1 cup mashed, very
    ripe bananas

5ml/1 tsp vanilla essence

60ml/4 tbsp milk

75g/3oz/¾ cup chopped walnuts

lemon-rind curls, to decorate

For the icing

115g/4oz/½ cup butter, at
    room temperature

450g/1lb/4½ cups icing sugar

5ml/1 tsp grated lemon rind

45–75ml/3–5 tbsp lemon juice

Preheat the oven to 180°C/350°F/Gas 4. Grease two 23cm/9in round cake tins and line the base of each with non-stick baking paper. Sift the flour, baking powder and salt into a bowl.

Beat the butter and sugars in a large mixing bowl until light and fluffy. Beat in the eggs, one at a time, then stir in the lemon rind.

Mix the mashed bananas with the vanilla essence and milk in a small bowl. Stir this, in batches, into the creamed butter mixture, alternating with the sifted flour. Stir lightly until just blended. Fold in the walnuts.

Divide the mixture between the cake tins and spread evenly. Bake for 30–35 minutes, until a skewer inserted in the centre comes out clean. Leave to stand for 5 minutes before turning out on to a wire rack. Peel off the lining paper and leave to cool.

Make the icing. Cream the butter in a bowl until smooth, then gradually beat in the icing sugar. Stir in the lemon rind and enough of the lemon juice to make a spreading consistency.

Place one of the cakes on a serving plate. Spread over one-third of the icing, then top with the second cake. Spread the remaining icing evenly over the top and sides of the cake. Decorate with lemon-rind curls.

BANANA NUT BREAD

Banana bread is always popular. This delicious, healthy version has added pecan nuts.

Makes 1 loaf

*115g/4oz/½ cup unsalted butter, at
    room temperature*
115g/4oz/½ cup granulated sugar
2 eggs, at room temperature
115g/4oz/1 cup plain flour
5ml/1 tsp bicarbonate of soda
1.5ml/¼ tsp salt
5ml/1 tsp ground cinnamon
50g/2oz/½ cup wholemeal flour
3 large ripe bananas
5ml/1 tsp vanilla essence
50g/2oz/½ cup pecan nuts, chopped

COOK'S TIP
*If the cake mixture shows signs
of curdling when you add the
eggs, beat in a little of the sifted
flour mixture.*

Preheat the oven to 180°C/350°F/Gas 4. Line the bottom and sides of a 23 x 13cm/9 x 5in loaf tin with non-stick baking paper.

Using an electric mixer, cream the butter and sugar in a bowl until light and fluffy. Add the eggs, one at a time, beating well after each addition.

Sift the plain flour, bicarbonate of soda, salt and cinnamon over the butter mixture. Stir in thoroughly, then stir in the wholemeal flour.

Mash the bananas to a purée and stir into the mixture. Stir in the vanilla essence and pecan nuts. Pour into the prepared tin and level the surface.

Bake the loaf for 50–60 minutes, until a skewer inserted in the centre comes out clean. Turn out on to a wire rack to cool.

GLAZED BANANA SPICE LOAF

Bananas and spices are perfect partners in this delicious loaf, which makes an ideal teatime treat.

Makes 1 loaf

1 large ripe banana

115g/4oz/½ cup butter, at room
  temperature

150g/5oz caster sugar

2 eggs, at room temperature

200g/7oz plain flour

5ml/1 tsp salt

5ml/1 tsp bicarbonate of soda

2.5ml/½ tsp grated nutmeg

1.5ml/¼ tsp ground allspice

1.5ml/¼ tsp ground cloves

175ml/6fl oz/¾ cup soured cream

5ml/1 tsp vanilla essence

For the glaze

115g/4oz icing sugar

15–30ml/1–2 tbsp lemon juice

Preheat the oven to 180°C/350°F/Gas 4. Line a 21.5 x 11.5cm/8½ x 4½in loaf tin with greaseproof paper and lightly grease. Using a fork, mash the banana in a bowl. Set aside. With an electric mixer, cream the butter and sugar until light and fluffy. Add the eggs, one at a time, beating well after each addition.

Sift together the flour, salt, bicarbonate of soda, nutmeg, allspice and cloves. Add to the butter mixture and mix well. Add the soured cream, banana and vanilla essence and mix just enough to blend. Pour into the prepared tin. Bake for 45–50 minutes, until the top springs back when touched. Cool in the tin for 10 minutes, then leave on a wire rack to cool.

For the glaze, mix the icing sugar and lemon juice, stirring until smooth. Place the cooled loaf on a rack set over a baking sheet. Pour the glaze over the top of the loaf and allow to set.

Hot Desserts

Cooked bananas have a sweetness and melting texture in delicious dishes such as crisp deep-fried bananas, hot bananas spiced with rum and cinnamon and pancakes with lime and maple syrup or with chocolate chips and toasted almonds.

BANANA MANDAZIS

These delicious banana fritters come from Africa, where they are very popular.

Serves 4

1 egg

2 ripe bananas, roughly chopped

150ml/¼ pint/⅔ cup milk

2.5ml/½ tsp vanilla essence

225g/8oz/2 cups self-raising flour

5ml/1 tsp baking powder

45ml/3 tbsp granulated sugar

vegetable oil, for deep-frying

icing sugar, for dusting

COOK'S TIP

Drain each batch of mandazis well on kitchen paper and keep them hot in a low oven while you are cooking the remainder.

Place the egg, bananas, milk, vanilla essence, flour, baking powder and sugar in a blender or food processor. Process to a smooth, creamy batter. If it is too thick, add a little extra milk. Set aside for 10 minutes.

Heat the oil in a heavy-based saucepan or deep-fat fryer. When hot, carefully place spoonfuls of the mixture in the oil and fry for 3–4 minutes until golden. Remove with a slotted spoon and drain well. Keep hot while cooking the remaining mandazis. Dust with icing sugar and serve at once.

HOT BANANAS WITH RUM AND RAISINS

Choose almost-ripe bananas with evenly coloured skins, either all yellow or just green only at the tips.
Black patches indicate that the fruit is over-ripe.

Serves 4

40g/1½oz/¼ cup seedless raisins

75ml/5 tbsp dark rum

50g/2oz/4 tbsp unsalted butter

60ml/4 tbsp soft light brown sugar

4 ripe bananas, peeled and
*   halved lengthways*

1.5ml/¼ tsp grated nutmeg

1.5ml/¼ tsp ground cinnamon

30ml/2 tbsp slivered almonds, toasted

chilled cream or vanilla ice cream, to
*   serve (optional)*

Put the raisins in a bowl and pour over the rum. Leave to soak for about 30 minutes, by which time the raisins will have plumped up.

Melt the butter in a frying pan, add the brown sugar and stir until just dissolved. Add the bananas and cook them for 4–5 minutes until they are just tender.

Sprinkle the nutmeg and cinnamon over the bananas, then pour over the rum and raisins. Stand back and carefully set the rum alight, using a long taper, and stir gently to mix.

Scatter the slivered almonds over the bananas and serve immediately with chilled cream or vanilla ice cream, if you like. Crème fraîche or Greek-style yogurt would also make a delicious accompaniment for the bananas.

VARIATION

Use sultanas soaked in a tangerine-flavoured liqueur, such as Van der Hum, or an orange-flavoured liqueur, such as Grand Marnier, instead of raisins in rum.

SPICED NUTTY BANANAS

Baked bananas are delectable however you serve them, but with a triple nut topping they are delicious.

Serves 3

6 ripe, but firm, bananas

*30ml/2 tbsp chopped, unsalted
    cashew nuts*

*30ml/2 tbsp chopped, unsalted
    peanuts*

30ml/2 tbsp desiccated coconut

15ml/1 tbsp demerara sugar

5ml/1 tsp ground cinnamon

2.5ml/½ tsp freshly grated nutmeg

150ml/¼ pint/⅔ cup orange juice

60ml/4 tbsp rum

15g/½oz/1 tbsp butter or margarine

*double cream or Greek-style yogurt,
    to serve*

COOK'S TIP
*Freshly grated nutmeg makes
all the difference to this dish.
You can add more rum, if you
like, and chopped mixed nuts
can be used instead of unsalted
peanuts.*

Preheat the oven to 200°C/400°F/Gas 6. Slice the bananas and place in a large, greased, shallow ovenproof dish. Do not leave for long at this stage as the bananas will discolour.

Mix the cashew nuts, peanuts, coconut, sugar, cinnamon and nutmeg in a small bowl. Pour the orange juice and rum over the bananas, then sprinkle evenly with the nut and sugar mixture.

Dot the top evenly with butter or margarine. Bake for 15–20 minutes or until the bananas are golden brown and the sauce is bubbling.

Serve the bananas hot, with double cream or Greek-style yogurt.

BANANAS FOSTER

Possibly the most famous banana dessert, this originated in the French Quarter of New Orleans.

Serves 4

75g/3oz/⅓ cup soft light brown sugar

2.5ml/½ tsp ground cinnamon

2.5ml/½ tsp grated nutmeg

50g/2oz/4 tbsp unsalted butter

60ml/4 tbsp banana liqueur

75ml/5 tbsp dark rum

4 firm bananas

4 scoops firmly frozen vanilla
   ice cream

VARIATION
You can ring the changes with praline, walnut or even rum-and-raisin ice cream.

Mix the sugar, cinnamon and nutmeg in a bowl. Melt the butter in a heavy-based frying pan and add the sugar and spice mixture, with the liqueur and rum. Stir over the heat until the sauce is syrupy.

Peel the bananas, cut them in half lengthways and add them to the pan. Heat through, turning to coat with the sauce.

Tilt the pan if you are cooking over gas to set light to the sauce. If your stove is electric, light the sauce with a long-handled match. Hold the pan at arm's length while you do this.

As soon as the flames die down, put some pieces of banana on each plate, with a scoop of ice cream. Pour on the sauce and serve immediately.

DEEP-FRIED BANANAS

An Indonesian speciality, deep-fried bananas make a splendid spur-of-the-moment dessert.

Serves 8

115g/4oz/1 cup self-raising flour

40g/1½oz/¼ cup rice flour

2.5ml/½ tsp salt

200ml/7fl oz/scant 1 cup water

finely grated lime rind (optional)

8 small bananas

oil for deep-frying

caster sugar, for dredging

1 lime, cut in wedges, to serve

Sift both the flours and the salt together into a bowl. Add just enough water to make a smooth, coating batter. Mix well, then add the lime rind, if using.

Heat the oil to 190°C/375°F or until a cube of day-old bread browns in 30 seconds. Peel the bananas and dip them into the batter two or three times. Deep-fry until crisp and golden.

Drain the bananas, and transfer them to a plate. Dredge with caster sugar and serve hot, with the lime wedges.

COOK'S TIP

Cook these delicious deep-fried bananas at the last minute before serving, so the crust is still crisp while the centre stays melt-in-the-mouth soft.

BANANA, MAPLE AND LIME PANCAKES

Pancakes are a treat any day of the week, especially when they are filled with bananas and maple syrup.

Serves 4

115g/4oz/1 cup plain flour

1 egg white

250ml/8fl oz/1 cup milk

sunflower oil, for frying

strips of lime rind, to decorate

For the filling

4 bananas, sliced

45ml/3 tbsp maple syrup or
*   golden syrup*

30ml/2 tbsp fresh lime juice

Mix the flour, egg white and milk in a bowl. Add 60ml/4 tbsp cold water and whisk until smooth and bubbly. Chill until needed.

Heat a little oil in a non-stick frying pan and swirl in enough batter just to coat the base. Cook until golden, then turn over and cook the other side. Keep hot while making the remaining pancakes.

Make the filling. Place the bananas, syrup and lime juice in a pan and simmer gently for 1 minute. Spoon into the pancakes and fold into quarters. Sprinkle with strips of lime rind to decorate.

COOK'S TIP
Pancakes freeze well. To store for later use, stack and interleave them with non-stick baking paper, overwrap with foil and freeze for up to 3 months. Thaw thoroughly and reheat before using.

CHOCOLATE CHIP BANANA PANCAKES

Serve these delicious banana pancakes as a dessert topped with cream and toasted almonds.

Makes 16

2 ripe bananas

200ml/7fl oz/scant 1 cup milk

2 eggs

150g/5oz/1¼ cups self-raising flour

25g/1oz/⅓ cup ground almonds

15ml/1 tbsp caster sugar

25g/1oz/3 tbsp plain chocolate chips

butter, for frying

pinch of salt

For the topping

150ml/¼ pint/⅔ cup double cream

15ml/1 tbsp icing sugar

50g/2oz/½ cup toasted flaked almonds

VARIATION

For banana and blueberry pancakes, replace the chocolate chips with 115g/4oz/1 cup fresh blueberries. Hot pancakes are simply delicious served with ice cream.

In a bowl, mash the bananas with a fork. Mix in half of the milk, then beat in the eggs. Sift in the flour and add the ground almonds, sugar and salt. Mix lightly. Add the remaining milk and stir in the chocolate chips to produce a thick batter.

Heat a knob of butter in a large, non-stick frying pan. Spoon the pancake mixture into heaps, allowing room for them to spread. When bubbles appear on top of the pancakes, turn them over and cook briefly on the other side. Remove and keep hot.

Whip the cream lightly with the icing sugar. Spoon on to the pancakes and top each with a few flaked almonds.

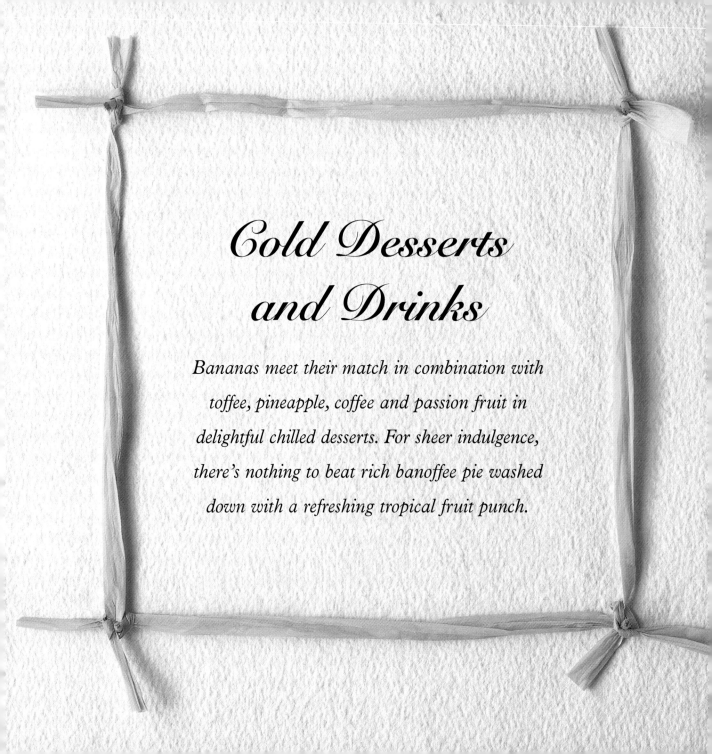

Cold Desserts and Drinks

Bananas meet their match in combination with toffee, pineapple, coffee and passion fruit in delightful chilled desserts. For sheer indulgence, there's nothing to beat rich banoffee pie washed down with a refreshing tropical fruit punch.

BANANA AND MELON IN ORANGE VANILLA SAUCE

A chilled banana and melon compote in a delicious orange sauce makes a perfect summer dessert.

Serves 4

300ml/½ pint/1¼ cups orange juice

1 vanilla pod

5ml/1 tsp finely grated orange rind

15ml/1 tbsp granulated sugar

4 ripe but firm bananas

1 honeydew melon

30ml/2 tbsp lemon juice

*strips of blanched orange rind, to
    garnish (optional)*

COOK'S TIP

*Most large supermarkets and
health food shops sell vanilla
pods, and you can wash, dry
and store them for re-use. If
unavailable, use a few drops of
vanilla essence instead.*

Place the orange juice in a small saucepan with the vanilla pod, orange rind and sugar. Heat gently, stirring until the sugar has dissolved, then bring to the boil.

Lower the heat and simmer gently for 15 minutes or until the sauce is syrupy. Remove from the heat and leave to cool. Remove the vanilla pod. If using vanilla essence, stir it into the sauce once it has cooled.

Roughly chop the bananas and melon, place in a large serving bowl and toss with the lemon juice. Pour the cooled sauce over and chill the compote. Decorate with the blanched orange rind, if using, before serving.

BRAZILIAN COFFEE BANANAS

Rich, lavish and sinful-looking, this banana dessert takes only moments to make.

Serves 4

4 small ripe bananas

*15ml/1 tbsp instant coffee granules
   or powder*

30ml/2 tbsp dark muscovado sugar

*250g/9oz/generous 1 cup Greek-
   style yogurt*

15ml/1 tbsp toasted flaked almonds

VARIATION

*For a special occasion, add a
dash of dark rum, brandy or
crème de cacao to the bananas
for extra richness.*

Peel and slice one banana. Peel and mash the remaining three in a bowl with a fork. Dissolve the coffee in 15ml/1 tbsp boiling water and stir into the mashed bananas.

Spoon a little of the mashed banana mixture into four serving dishes and sprinkle with sugar. Top with a spoonful of yogurt, then repeat the layers until all the ingredients are used up.

Using a skewer or cocktail stick, swirl the last layer of yogurt for a marbled effect. Finish with a few banana slices and flaked almonds. Serve cold, preferably within an hour of making.

QUICK BANANA PUDDING

For instant energy and excellent taste, tuck into this simple banana pudding with a caramel topping.

Serves 6–8

4 thick slices of ginger cake

6 ripe bananas

30ml/2 tbsp lemon juice

300ml/½ pint/1¼ cups
whipping cream

60ml/4 tbsp orange juice

30–45ml/2–3 tbsp soft light
brown sugar

VARIATION

You could use fromage frais
instead of whipping cream if
you prefer. However, do not try
to whip it – simply stir in half
the recommended amount of
fruit juice.

Break up the cake into chunks and arrange in an ovenproof dish. Slice the bananas into a bowl and toss with the lemon juice.

Whip the cream in a separate bowl until firm, then gently whip in the juice. Fold in the bananas and spoon the mixture over the ginger cake.

Top with the sugar, sprinkling it in an even layer. Place under a hot grill for 2–3 minutes to caramelize. Chill in the refrigerator until set firm again, if you wish, or serve at once.

FLUFFY BANANA AND PINEAPPLE MOUSSE

This light, low-fat banana mousse looks very impressive but is extremely easy to make.

Serves 6

2 ripe bananas

225g/8oz/1 cup cottage cheese

425g/15oz can pineapple chunks or
  pieces in juice

15ml/1 tbsp/1 sachet powdered
  gelatine

2 egg whites

COOK'S TIP

For a simpler way of serving,
use a 1-litre/1¾-pint/4-cup
serving dish, which will hold
all the mixture, and do not tie
a collar around the edge.
Decorate the top with the
reserved banana and pineapple
as described in the recipe.

Tie a double band of non-stick baking paper around a 600-ml/1-pint/2½-cup soufflé dish to come 5cm/2in above the rim. Peel and chop one banana and place it in a food processor with the cottage cheese. Process until smooth.

Drain the pineapple, saving the juice and setting aside a few pieces for decoration. Add the rest of the pineapple to the mixture in the processor and process for a few seconds until finely chopped.

Pour 60ml/4 tbsp of the reserved pineapple juice into a small heatproof bowl and sprinkle the gelatine on top. When spongy, place over simmering water, stirring until the gelatine has dissolved. Stir the gelatine quickly into the fruit mixture. Whisk the egg whites to soft peaks. Fold them into the mixture. Tip the mousse mixture into the prepared dish, smooth the surface and chill until set. Carefully remove the paper collar. Slice the remaining banana and use it with the reserved pineapple to decorate the mousse.

BOSTON BANOFFEE PIE

Guaranteed to bring a grin to diners' faces, this is a winning combination of bananas and toffee.

Makes a 20cm/8in pie

20cm/8in cooked pastry case, cooled

2 small bananas, sliced

a little lemon juice

whipped cream and grated plain
*   chocolate, to decorate*

For the filling

115g/4oz/½ cup butter

½ x 400g/14oz can sweetened
*   condensed milk*

115g/4oz/⅔ cup soft light brown sugar

30ml/2 tbsp golden syrup

COOK'S TIP

To make the pastry case, rub
115g/4oz/½ cup butter into
150g/5oz/1¼ cups plain flour.
Stir in 60ml/4 tbsp caster sugar
and press into a 20cm/8in flan
tin. Fill with crumpled foil and
bake at 160°C/325°F/Gas 3
for 20–25 minutes.

Make the filling. Place the butter, condensed milk, brown sugar and golden syrup in a large non-stick saucepan. Heat gently, stirring occasionally, until the sugar has dissolved.

Bring to a gentle boil and cook for 7 minutes, stirring all the time (to prevent burning), until the mixture thickens and turns a light caramel colour. Pour into the cooked pastry case and leave until cold.

Decorate with the bananas dipped in the lemon juice. Pipe a swirl of whipped cream in the centre and sprinkle with the grated chocolate.

TROPICAL BANANA FRUIT SALAD

Not surprisingly, bananas go particularly well with other tropical fruits.

Serves 4–6

1 medium pineapple

400g/14oz can guava halves
 in syrup

1 large mango, peeled, stoned
 and diced

2 medium bananas

115g/4oz/⅔ cup stem ginger, plus
 30ml/2 tbsp of the syrup

60ml/4 tbsp thick coconut milk

10ml/2 tsp granulated sugar

2.5ml/½ tsp grated nutmeg

2.5ml/½ tsp ground cinnamon

strips of fresh coconut, to decorate

COOK'S TIP

*For an appealing decorative
touch, use two small
pineapples. Cut them in half,
through the leaves, carefully
scoop out the pulp and use the
shells as containers for the
tropical fruit salad.*

Peel the pineapple, remove the core, cut the flesh into cubes and place in a large serving bowl. Drain the guavas, reserving the syrup, and chop them into dice. Add the guavas and mango to the bowl. Slice one of the bananas and add it to the bowl.

Chop the stem ginger and add it to the pineapple mixture. Mix together lightly. Pour the ginger syrup into a blender or food processor. Add the reserved guava syrup, coconut milk and sugar. Slice the remaining banana and add to the mixture. Blend to a smooth, creamy purée.

Pour the banana and coconut purée over the fruit, add a little freshly grated nutmeg and a good sprinkling of the ground cinnamon. Serve the fruit salad chilled, decorated with strips of coconut.

BANANA HONEY YOGURT ICE

Smooth and silky, this delicious banana ice is very refreshing when eaten after a rich meal.

Serves 4-6

4 ripe bananas, roughly chopped

15ml/1 tbsp lemon juice

30ml/2 tbsp clear honey

*250g/9oz/generous 1 cup Greek-
    style yogurt*

2.5ml/½ tsp ground cinnamon

*crisp biscuits, flaked hazelnuts and
    banana slices, to serve*

Place the bananas in a food processor or blender with the lemon juice, honey, yogurt and cinnamon. Process until smooth and creamy.

Pour the mixture into a suitable container for freezing and freeze until almost solid. Spoon back into the food processor and process the mixture again until smooth.

Return the yogurt ice to the freezer until firm. Before serving, allow the ice to soften at room temperature for 15 minutes. Scoop into individual bowls and serve with crisp biscuits, flaked hazelnuts and banana slices.

COOK'S TIP

Switch the freezer to the coldest setting about an hour before making the yogurt ice to ensure that it freezes quickly.

BANANA AND PASSION FRUIT WHIP

Creamy mashed bananas combine beautifully with passion fruit in this easy and quickly prepared dessert.

Serves 4

2 ripe bananas

2 passion fruit

90ml/6 tbsp fromage frais

150ml/¼ pint/⅔ cup double cream

10ml/2 tsp clear honey

shortcake or ginger biscuits, to serve

COOK'S TIP

Look out for cans of passion fruit (or grenadilla) pulp. Use with sliced banana and whipped cream to make a marvellous topping for pavlova or for sandwiching together individual meringues.

Slice the bananas into a bowl then, using a fork, mash them to a smooth purée. Cut the passion fruit in half. Using a teaspoon, scoop the pulp into the bowl. Add the fromage frais and mix gently.

In a separate bowl, whip the cream with the honey until it forms soft peaks. Carefully fold the cream and honey mixture into the fruit. Spoon into four glass dishes and serve the whip at once, with the biscuits.

BREAD AND BANANA YOGURT ICE

Serve this tempting yogurt ice with strawberries and biscuits for a luscious, light dessert.

Serves 6

115g/4oz/2 cups fresh
   wholemeal breadcrumbs
50g/2oz/⅓ cup soft light brown sugar
300ml/½ pint/1¾ cups ready-made
   cold custard
150g/5oz fromage frais
150ml/¼ pint/⅔ cup Greek-
   style yogurt
4 bananas
juice of 1 lemon
25g/1oz/¼ cup icing sugar, sifted
50g/2oz/½ cup raisins, chopped
pared lemon rind, to decorate
fresh strawberries, halved, to serve

Preheat the oven to 200°C/400°F/Gas 6. Mix the breadcrumbs and brown sugar in a bowl. Spread the mixture out on a non-stick baking sheet. Bake for about 10 minutes until the crumbs are crisp, stirring occasionally. Set aside to cool.

Meanwhile, mix the custard, fromage frais and yogurt in a bowl. Mash the bananas with the lemon juice and add to the custard mixture, mixing well. Fold in the icing sugar.

Pour the mixture into a shallow, freezerproof container and freeze for about 3 hours or until mushy in consistency. Spoon into a chilled bowl and quickly mash with a fork to break down the ice crystals.

Add the breadcrumbs and raisins and mix well. Return the mixture to the container, cover and freeze until firm. Serve with the strawberries, if using, decorated with lemon rind.

COOK'S TIP

Transfer the ice to the refrigerator about 30 minutes before serving to allow it to soften a little. This will make it easier to scoop neatly so that it looks attractive when served.

BANANA FRUIT PUNCH

This pleasingly quick and simple Caribbean speciality is perfect for a summer party.

Serves 3–4

2 bananas

60ml/4 tbsp ginger syrup

2.5ml/½ tsp almond essence

2.5ml/½ tsp vanilla essence

1 litre/1¾ pints/4 cups mango juice

750ml/1¼ pints/3 cups
   pineapple juice

250ml/8fl oz/1 cup lemonade

freshly grated nutmeg

lemon balm and orange slices, to
   decorate

Chop the bananas into 1cm/½in pieces. Place them in a blender or food processor. Add the ginger syrup and essences and process until smooth.

Transfer the mixture to a large punch bowl. Stir in the mango and pineapple juices, then pour in the lemonade. Finish by sprinkling in some grated nutmeg. Serve chilled, decorated with lemon balm and orange slices.

COOK'S TIP
*Prepare this punch up to
2 hours in advance of serving
and chill until ready to
decorate and serve.*

DEMERARA RUM AND BANANA PUNCH

The inspiration for this punch came from Guyana, where bananas, rum and unrefined sugar are used to make a variety of potent drinks. Use any combination of fruits to decorate the punch.

Serves 4

150ml/¼ pint/⅔ cup orange juice

150ml/¼ pint/⅔ cup pineapple juice

150ml/¼ pint/⅔ cup mango juice

250ml/8fl oz/1 cup dark rum

a shake of angostura bitters

freshly grated nutmeg

25g/1oz/2 tbsp demerara sugar

1 small banana

1 large orange, sliced

COOK'S TIP

Demerara rum from Guyana is traditional, but you can use white rum, if you prefer. For an alcohol-free version, use ginger ale instead of rum.

Pour the orange, pineapple and mango juices into a large punch bowl. Stir in 120ml/4fl oz/½ cup water and add the rum, angostura bitters, nutmeg and sugar. Stir gently for a few minutes until the sugar has dissolved.

Slice the banana and stir gently into the punch. Float the orange slices on top. Chill and serve with ice.

INDEX